History
of the
Society of the Friendly Sons
of
St. Patrick
of
Washington, D. C.
1928 - 1968

by

EDWARD T. FOLLIARD

Historian of The Society

March 1968

FOREWORD

Our Society of the Friendly Sons of St. Patrick is not old, not young. It is certainly not old compared to the parent organization in Philadelphia, which antedates the Republic, itself. Yet, at the age of 40, it is no fledgling either. The four decades of its existence have been the most exciting the world has ever known. The City of Washington has been transformed from a rather somnolent town to a world capital. What we now call Metropolitan or Greater Washington has spread out over vast areas of farmland in Maryland and Virginia, and the population has doubled, trebled, and then some.

The Society of the Friendly Sons of St. Patrick has reflected the changes, naturally; but above all it has sought to fulfill its aim of promoting "better relations among all peoples" and adding a little gaiety to life. Our Fortieth Anniversary year, it seemed to me, was a good time for retrospection, a good time for a summing up. Hence, this provisional history by the Society's Historian, Edward T. Folliard, for many years a White House correspondent and 1947 winner of the Pulitzer Prize for national reporting.

HONORABLE WILLIAM B. JONES
President of The Society of the
Friendly Sons of St. Patrick of
Washington, D. C.—1967-1968

The Apostle of the Gael

FOUNDING OF THE SOCIETY

The Society of the Friendly Sons of St. Patrick of Washington, D. C., is now 40 years old, having been founded in 1928. Thus it may be said to have reached maturity. But it is, of course, an offspring; and to appreciate its noble lineage and the spirit that animates it, one must go back to March 17, 1771, when the Society of the Friendly Sons of St. Patrick was born in Philadelphia, Pa., then the largest city in the American colonies.

Stephen Moylan, first president of the Friendly Sons, was a native of Cork whose mother was the Countess of Limerick. He was an aide to General George Washington at the seige of Boston, and later was quartermaster general of the Continental Army. He resigned from that post to organize the Irish Dragoons, an outfit which took part in many battles and endured that awful winter with General Washington at Valley Forge.

Other charter (or early) members of the Friendly Sons who distinguished themselves in the American Revolution were General Anthony (Mad Anthony) Wayne, Commodore John Barry, General Edward Hand, Richard Bache, Dr. John Cochran, Colonel Turlbutt Francis, Tench Francis, Sharp Delaney, General Henry Knox, John Lardner, Thomas FitzSimons, John Boyle, and General Michael Morgan O'Brien.

One of the honorary members of the Society at that time was Robert Morris, "Financier of the Revolution."

At the first banquet of the Friendly Sons, "Patriotism" and "Charity" were proclaimed as the Society's cardinal principles. The design of the gold medal of the Society, approved in 1772, bespeaks love for Ireland and the then British crown colony of America: "On the right, Hibernia; on the left America; in the center, Liberty joining the hands of Hibernia and America, represented by the usual figure of a female supported by a harp for Hibernia; an Indian with his quiver on his back and his bow low slung, for America. Underneath, Unite. On the reverse St. Patrick, trampling on a snake, a cross in his hand, dressed in his pontifical robes. The motto—Hier." (This same medal, suspended from a green ribbon, is used by the Friendly Sons of Washington, D. C.)

GEORGE WASHINGTON

On December 18, 1781, the Friendly Sons of Philadelphia "adopted" General Washington as a member of the Society, thus making an Irishman out of him as far as it was within their power to do so. A delegation of the Friendly Sons, headed by President George Campbell, called on him at his headquarters, presented him with his gold medal and invited him to a dinner on January 1, 1782. General Washington, using the stately language of the day, accepted membership in these words:

> "I accept with singular pleasure the Ensign of so worthy a Fraternity as the Sons of St. Patrick of this city—a Society distinguished for the firm adherence of its members to the glorious cause in which we are embarked.

> "Give me leave to assure you, Sir, that I shall never cast my eyes upon the badge with which I am honored, but with a grateful remembrance of the polite and affectionate manner in which it was presented."

General Washington, in citing the Friendly Sons for their patriotism, may have been aware that the Society had, in 1775, expelled Thomas Batt, a Tory accused of "taking an active part against the liberty of America." Batt was the only black sheep of the flock, a remarkable record considering that nearly half of the population of the colonies was either Tory or neutral.

General Washington attended two dinners of the Friendly Sons on January 1 and on March 17 in 1782. Thomas Jefferson, Alexander Hamilton and John Paul Jones were among the famous men who turned out for dinners in honor of Ireland's patron saint in the post-war years.

Nearly all of the early members of the Society of the Friendly Sons in Philadelphia were prosperous merchants, many of them engaged in the shipping and importing business. That they were generous as well as affluent may be judged by something that happened in 1780. The Revolutionary War was still on, and General Washington was, as usual, desperately in need of money to pay the expenses of the Continental Army. We read in the annals of the time that 27 Friendly Sons, pledging their property and their credit, raised 103,500 pounds in Pennsylvania currency, payable in gold and silver, to help finance the war.

2

THE NEW YORK SOCIETY

Dr. John Cochran, who was surgeon general and director of hospitals for the Continental Army, and William Constable, who served as aide to the Marquis de Lafayette, helped to organize the Society of the Friendly Sons of St. Patrick in New York. The year was 1783. Among other charter members were George Clinton, first post-Revolution Governor of New York, and James Duane, first Mayor of New York City.

One of the most colorful members of the Society in New York at the time was a man whose story has long fascinated Judge Matthew F. McGuire. This fellow had the formidable name of Hercules Mulligan. He was a tailor. He was also General Washington's favorite spy. In the long British occupation of New York, Hercules Mulligan made uniforms for British officers; and in his fitting room, he picked up intelligence that was of great value to the Continental Army. General Washington, after entering New York in triumph, had breakfast at the home of Hercules, and thus protected him from the anger that was vented on many New York businessmen who had catered to the British.

Reporting on a dinner of the Friendly Sons of New York in Cape Tavern, at the foot of Broadway, on St. Patrick's Day, 1784, a newspaper said that "a number of suitable toasts were drunk upon this joyful occasion . . . and perhaps the great saint was never honored with a concourse of more generous and truly patriotic sons than this assembly afforded."

After the ratification of the Constitution and the establishment of the Republic, the Friendly Sons inaugurated the practice of offering their first toast at a banquet to "the President of the United States." This was just a beginning; then came toasts to the 13 original states. An attempt was made to increase the number of toasts with the addition of new states. However, a conservative element beat down the proposal, thus sparing modern Friendly Sons the challenge of rising to salute today's 50 states.

But at a time when bar whisky cost 3 cents a glass, the toasts were numerous and piquant, as for example:

"May the sons of liberty never want for roast beef or claret."

"To the land we left and the land we live in."

"To the friends of civil and religious liberty all over the world."

"To the memory of George Washington."

"To the memory of Andrew Jackson."

"The shamrock and the shillelagh—with the one we crown our mirth, with the other we drub our enemies."

And finally:

"To our noble selves."

The Society in New York, whose roster over the years has been adorned by the names of such men as Alfred E. Smith, Victor Herbert, and James A. (Big Jim) Farley, has 1000 members and a waiting list of more than 600. Some have been waiting more than 20 years.

From the beginning, the Society of the Friendly Sons of St. Patrick has been non-sectarian. It has scrupulously recognized the right of the individual to choose his religion according to the dictates of his conscience. This spirit was beautifully expressed by the Irish lyric poet, Thomas Moore (1779-1852), in a verse which always appears on the dinner programs of the Society in Philadelphia:

Shall I ask those brave soldiers who fight at my side
In the cause of mankind if our creeds agree?

Shall I give up the friend I have valued and tried,
If he kneel not before the same altar with me?

Thus, it might be said that the Society of the Friendly Sons of St. Patrick was a trail-blazer in what the world now acclaims as the ecumenical movement.

4

THE SOCIETY IN WASHINGTON, D. C.

Dublin-born Tom Moore, who in his time enjoyed a popularity second only to that of Lord Byron, is perhaps best known for "The Harp That Once Through Tara's Halls," "Believe Me, If All Those Endearing Young Charms," and " 'Tis the Last Rose of Summer." But Moore also wrote something about Washington, D. C., that has been quoted more often than any verse ever inspired by this city on the Potomac.

First, a little background on the city, borrowed from the late William P. Kennedy, Litt. D., first Historian of the Society of the Friendly Sons of St. Patrick of Washington, D. C. The area that is now the National Capital was inhabited by the Algonquin tribe before it was taken over by Irish and Scotch settlers late in the 17th Century. One of the early proprietors, Francis Pope, envisioned a city here that would rival ancient Rome. And so he called it Rome, and the name of the stream that flowed near the foot of Capitol Hill he changed from Goose Creek to the Tiber.

William P. Kennedy

Tom Moore, visiting Washington in 1804, heard of Francis Pope's dream and memorialized it in these delightful lines:

"In fancy now, 'neath the twilight gloom,
Come, let me lead thee o'er the second Rome,
Where tribunes rule, where dusky Davi bow,
Where what was Goose Creek once is Tiber now;
This embryo Capital, where fancy sees
Squares in morasses, obelisks in trees
Which second-sighted seers, even now adorn
With shrines unbuilt to heroes yet unborn."

Now we pick up Historian Kennedy's story of the laying out of the city named after the man "adopted" by the Friendly Sons of St. Patrick in 1781:

"One of the three Commissioners appointed by Washington to take charge of defining the boundaries and surveying the site of the Federal City was Daniel Carroll, a cousin of Charles Carroll of Carrollton, one of the signers of the Declaration of Independence."

5

"Daniel Carroll was a brother of Bishop John Carroll, founder of Georgetown University. He himself was a member of the Continental Congress, a delegate to the convention that framed the Federal Constitution, and a member of the First Congress. . . .

"After Washington had personally selected the location for the President's House, it was a young Irishman born in Dublin, James Hoban, who in a competition was awarded, on July 17, 1792, the prize of $500 and a building lot for his plans for the original 'White House.' Hoban's plans are said to have been based upon the palace of the Duke of Leinster in Dublin."

There is a widespread notion that virtually all Americans of Irish blood trace their ancestry back to those who left Ireland at the time of the great potato famine of the 1840's. The fact is, of course, that the Irish (from the North and South) were among the first immigrants to cross the Atlantic in large numbers. Even before the American Revolution, they were coming over at the rate of 3000 a year.

The Irish certainly were around at the founding of Washington, D. C. Probably the first big celebration of St. Patrick's Day here came in 1802 when the "Sons of Hibernia" paraded through the town wearing shamrocks in their hatbands. A visitor from Paris, writing about a sojourn in Washington at that time, told of seeing this sign in one of the shops: "Peter Rodgers, saddler, from the green fields of Erin and Tyranny to the green streets of Washington and Liberty."

Irish labor played an important, perhaps a dominant part in the construction work and in the laying out of L'Enfant's system of broad streets and avenues of the new city.

On St. Patrick's Day, 1812, "a number of natives of Ireland and their American friends" celebrated at a banquet. An organization called the "Sons of Erin" gathered for a banquet that same year, and again on St. Patrick's Day, 1813, when one of the toasts was: "Columbia, the land of our choice, because it is the land of liberty—dear to us is that freedom we participate in, and for its preservation Irishmen will risk their all."

Yet it was not until 128 years after the government was moved to Washington—157 years after the parent organization was born in Philadelphia—that the Society of the Friendly Sons of St. Patrick came into being in the National Capital.

The pioneers in the move to form the Washington Society were: Daniel J. O'Brien, Peter A. Drury, William E. Leahy, Colonel Arthur O'Brien, the Rev. John J. Callaghan, Edward J. Walsh and Hugh Reilly. These seven called in Colonel William J. (Wild Bill) Donovan, Joseph P. Tumulty and George O'Connor, and all then became members of a committee that set about the work of organizing the Friendly Sons.

This committee of ten invited "a selected group of men of Irish blood" to attend a meeting in the Mayflower Hotel on Wednesday, April 18, 1928, and it was on this occasion that the Society of the Friendly Sons of St. Patrick of Washington, D. C. was formally launched.

The purpose of the organization was: "To foster and promote a knowledge of Irish culture and traditions; to keep alive the Celtic love for art, letters and history; to stimulate fellowship and good feeling among people of Irish extraction and lineage, and in every way to encourage, stimulate and strengthen better relations between all peoples."

It was a happy time to be born, that spring of 1928. Washington was abloom, the Coolidge bull market was going strong, and hardly any cannon were being fired in anger, anywhere. True, there was the 18th Amendment and the Volstead Act, but, as was being said at the time, the drys had their law and the wets had their liquor— and that was that.

On April 25, 1928, the Society held its second meeting to hear a report of the Committee on Organization and By-Laws, presented by Joseph P. Tumulty. This was approved, and the Society then elected these officers:

> *President*—Colonel Arthur O'Brien
> *First Vice President*—Herbert T. Shannon
> *Second Vice President*—William E. Leahy
> *Treasurer*—Daniel J. O'Brien
> *Secretary*—Milton E. Ailes, Jr.

COL. ARTHUR O'BRIEN

DANIEL J. O'BRIEN

WILLIAM E. LEAHY

JOSEPH P. TUMULTY

After his election, President O'Brien appointed an executive committee made up of Charles J. Bell, the Rev. Dr. Patrick J. Healy, Judge William DeLacy and Peter A. Drury.

Besides the officers and committee members, the Charter Members of the Society were:

John A. Brickley	Martin J. McNamara
The Rev. John J. Callaghan	Camden R. McAtee
Dr. H. J. Crosson	C. C. McChord
Thomas R. Crowley	Daniel J. O'Brien
Charles W. Darr	George H. O'Connor
Clarence F. Donohoe	Frank O'Hara
David J. Dunigan	J. W. O'Rourke
Leo K. Drury	Henry I. Quinn
John K. M. Ewing	Joseph A. Rafferty
John F. Finerty	Hugh Reilly
Edward P. Harrington	Leo A. Rover
Dr. P. J. Lennox	Joseph D. Sullivan
Thomas J. Mangan, Jr.	Joseph P. Tumulty

Edward J. Walsh

FOOD, ELOQUENCE, MIRTH

The first banquet of the Washington Society was held on the evening of Saturday, March 16, 1929, with Colonel O'Brien presiding. The orators were Senator Samuel M. Shortridge of California, John F. Crosby and Dr. Henry A. Lappin. Colin O'Moore, a noted Irish tenor, the Georgetown University Glee Club and the Mayflower Hotel Orchestra provided the music.

The banquet was held in the main ballroom of the Mayflower, and Dennis E. Connell later recalled in a memoir that many ladies were present. Connell wrote that this was the last time the fair sex was ever permitted to celebrate "The Day" with the Society, and he thought it "a pity." However, the "Players" of the Friendly Sons, for many years, repeated the show for the benefit of the Milk Fund, and many of the ladies enjoyed this. In 1967 the Irish Ambassador and the Society combined in a reception for the members and their ladies at the Embassy, and it is hoped that this will be repeated with other affairs for the ladies.

A photograph of the second banquet, held on March 17, 1930, (see center of book) confirms that it was indeed "stag." It shows the members and their guests seated at long tables stretching the length of the Mayflower's Sapphire Room, later the Williamsburg Room. This was when men wore hard, stand-up, gates-ajar collars with their dinner jackets.

George O'Connor, a lawyer by profession and a great troubador by avocation, was chairman of the entertainment committee for this 1930 dinner. And he saw to it that the entertainment was different— the Society's own. Thomas W. Brahany, long a stalwart of the Society, wrote a musical play entitled "A Sprig of Green," the setting of which was the Ireland of the 1850's. The dialogue was interrupted frequently for songs, good old-fashioned Irish tunes.

George O'Connor and Tom Brahany had hit upon an entertainment idea that was to enliven the dinners of the Society for 34 years.

President Harry S. Truman was made an honorary member at the 1946 dinner; and true to his reputation, the Missouri warrior shot from the hip. James Francis Reilly gave the necrology at the dinner, eulogizing those Friendly Sons who had passed on. When Reilly finished, and while the lights were still out, Mr. Truman applauded his eloquence with vigorous handclapping. In the stillness, it was like thunder.

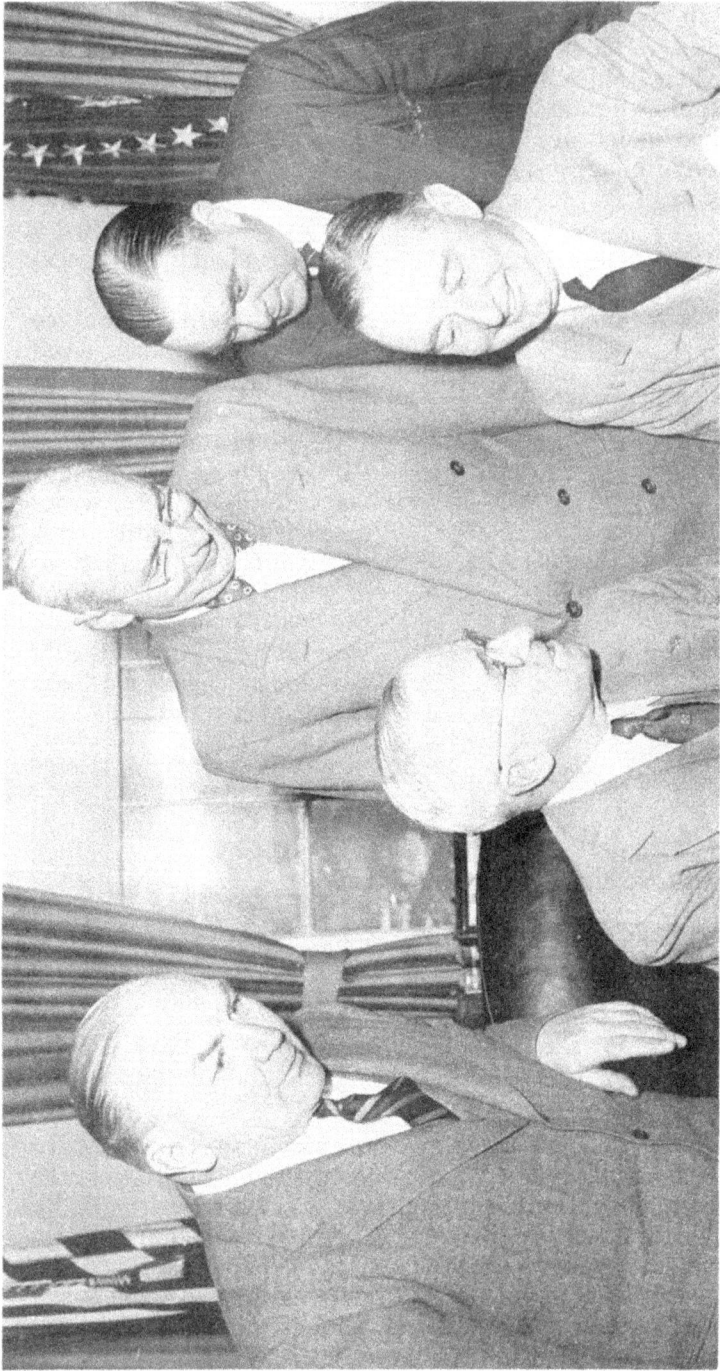

President Truman was well aware that many would think him guilty of a gaffe, but he was not the least upset. Grasping Reilly's hand, he said: "I don't care—that was a damn good job."

The orator of the evening at the 1946 dinner was a member of President Truman's "Little Cabinet"—John L. Sullivan, a member of the Society, who was then Assistant Secretary of the Navy and later Secretary of the Navy. He did something that most high-flying St. Patrick's Day orators find it almost impossible to do. He showed restraint.

It was 10 months after the end of World War II, and naturally Sullivan was expected to point to the valiant role of the Irish in that conflict, and to perhaps give the Irish credit for the victory.

> "I acknowledge a temptation to talk about Admiral Dan Callaghan, heroic Father Joe O'Callaghan, the Sullivan brothers, and many other heroes with Irish names and blood," Sullivan said. "Tonight I resist that temptation.
>
> "Yes, there were thousands of Kellys and Murphys and Sweeneys in every type of uniform. But we must remember that there were an equal number of Browns and Joneses. And a lot of Bernsteins and Cohens. . . ."

The dinner guests applauded, thus seeming to agree with Sullivan that the Irish had indeed required some help in beating Nazi Germany and Japan.

President Truman had earlier been a guest of honor at an extraordinary banquet of the Society. This was on November 24, 1945, the bicentennial of the birth of Commodore John Barry, "Father of the American Navy." James E. Colliflower presided, and introduced Mr. Truman.

> "I want to say to you," the President told the members and guests, "that it is the Irish in me which gives me the courage to try and do the job."

The Most Reverend Patrick A. O'Boyle was made an honorary member in 1948, three months after he came down from New York to be installed as Archbishop of Washington. In 1967, Pope Paul VI presented him with the red hat of a Cardinal, an honor that was acclaimed by all Washington, including the city's leading Protestant clergymen and Jewish Rabbis. Judge William Blakely Jones, 1967-1968 President of the Society, invited Cardinal O'Boyle to be the orator of the evening at the Fortieth Anniversary Dinner.

President Dwight D. Eisenhower was made an honorary member at the 1954 dinner, and it was President Howard W. Kacy who draped the green ribbon with its medallion around his neck.

SCHOLARSHIP—PROGRAM

In the winter of 1955, at the suggestion of Corneal J. Mack and Joseph P. Tumulty, Jr., the Society approved the Friendly Sons Exchange Fellowship Program as a means of "promoting good will between the peoples of the United States and Ireland."

To carry out the program, the Society organized a non-profit charitable Foundation with the same officers as the Society, itself. Initially a fund of $10,000 was subscribed. Thereafter, each member of the Society was to contribute $30 a year to the Foundation.

A delegation representing the Society, made up of Francis J. Kane, John A. Reilly and James A. Cassidy, journeyed to Ireland and talked to leading educators in Dublin and other centers of learning.

Since 1957, the Foundation has maintained a program for awarding two graduate fellowships, one for study in Ireland and the other for study in Washington. The fellowship for study in Ireland is awarded to a student, preferably of some Irish ancestry, who has been graduated from American University, Catholic University, Georgetown University or George Washington University. The student who wins the award has his choice of studying at the National University of Ireland, College of Dublin, Cork or Galway, the University of Dublin (Trinity College), or Queen's College in Belfast.

The fellowship for study in Washington is open to Irish students who are graduates of the aforementioned Irish universities, and provides for study in any of the aforementioned universities in Washington.

The awards cover up to three years of graduate study. At this stage, they amount to $2000 a year for study in Ireland and $3000 annually for study in Washington, a substantial increase over the original grants established in 1957, when the first awards were for $1200 and $1800.

Former President Tumulty, who is in charge of the program, reported in the spring of 1968 that up to then, nine young men had been awarded fellowships, four Americans and five Irish.

Chief Justice Earl Warren was made an honorary member in 1957. Over the years, he had an almost perfect record in attending the annual dinners.

President Eisenhower was again a guest at the 1959 dinner, when James Francis Reilly was the Society's president. This was a particularly memorable dinner because of the presence of another Chief of State, President Sean T. O'Kelly of Ireland. The Irish leader charmed all with his eloquence and wit, prompting Ike to say that he wished he could have had his help in the political campaigns of 1952 and 1956.

Said President O'Kelly:

"Nowhere, I venture to say, is St. Patrick's Day celebrated with greater enthusiasm than in the United States."

L BANQUET
OF THE
SAINT PATRICK
MARCH 17, 1930.

John Fitzgerald Kennedy was, of course, the most thoroughly Irish of all American Presidents, his great-grandfather, Patrick Kennedy, having come to the United States at the time of the famine in the 1840's. His great-grandfather on the maternal side came over about the same time. It was a case of embarrassment all around when on March 17, 1963, President Kennedy and his brother, Bobby, arrived at the Mayflower to attend the annual dinner of the Friendly Sons only to find that it had ended early and that the banquet hall was deserted. The terrible crime in Dallas on November 22, 1963, robbed the country of a President of great promise, and the Society of a chance to enroll him as an honorary member.

President Lyndon B. Johnson attended the 1966 dinner in the Statler-Hilton, and was inducted as an honorary member by the Rev. Dr. C. Leslie Glenn, S.T.D., the Society's president. LBJ recalled that 80 percent of the voters of Irish blood had supported him in the 1964 election.

> "I wonder what happened to the other 20 percent?" he asked.

The big Texan ended his talk with a "God bless you all," and on his way out shook hands with all those at the head table.

It was the second time in his administration that President Johnson had attended a dinner of the Friendly Sons. On March 17, 1964, four months after moving into the White House, he was the guest of honor at a dinner given by the New York Society in the Waldorf Astoria Hotel. The 2300 at the dinner gave him a big hand when he told them that he himself was "an Irishman by osmosis."

> "I woke up this morning," he said, "and suddenly realized that the Irish have taken over the government. And I like it. The Speaker of the House is a distinguished Irishman from Boston named John McCormack. The very effective majority leader of the Senate is an Irishman from Montana, Mike Mansfield."

> "And wherever I turn all day long there are Kenny O'Donnell and Larry O'Brien and Dave Powers and Dick McGuire and John Bailey and George Reedy and Ralph Dungan—the White House chapter of the Friendly Sons of St. Patrick."

19

20

At the time, of course, the so-called Irish Mafia, made up of Kennedy appointees, was still on the job in the White House.

It was a night of soaring oratory at the Waldorf, with one speaker after another taking wing, but President Johnson more than held his own when he ended his talk with the famous Gaelic toast:

> *May the road ever rise to*
> *meet you,*
> *May the wind ever be at*
> *your back.*
> *May you safely be in Heaven*
> *at least one hour before*
> *the Devil knows you're*
> *gone;*
> *And may the Good Lord*
> *always hold you in the*
> *hollow of His hand.*

Fortieth Anniversary Dinner

OFFICERS OF THE SOCIETY

1967-1968

Hon. William B. Jones
PRESIDENT

Robert W. Fleming
1ST VICE PRESIDENT

Hon. John L. Sullivan
2ND VICE PRESIDENT

Gerald K. Cassidy
TREASURER

John B. Cullen
SECRETARY

Edward T. Folliard
HISTORIAN

MEMBERS OF THE SOCIETY—1968

Argy, Dr. William P.
(Physician)

Argy, Dr. William P., Jr.
(Physician)

Baltz, Edward C.
(Chairman of the Board,
Perpetual Building Assn.)

Blunck, Herbert T.
(Senior Vice President,
Hilton Hotels Corp.)

Burke, Vincent C., Jr.
(Senior Vice President &
Trust Officer,
Riggs National Bank)

Burrus, George B.
(Chairman of the Board &
President,
Peoples Drug Stores, Inc.)

Cahill, Rev. Raymond P.
(Pastor, Our Lady of Mercy
Church)

Callahan, Daniel J., Jr.
(Farmer, Poolesville, Md.)

Callahan, Francis M.
(Attorney-at-Law)

Carmichael, Dr. Leonard
(Vice President, National
Geographic Society)

Carmody, John J.
(Attorney-at-Law)

Carmody, John J., Jr.
(Attorney-at-Law)

Carolan, Thomas H.
(Attorney-at-Law)

Cartwright, Rt. Rev. Msgr.,
John K., P.A.
(Retired)

Cassidy, Gerald K.
(Vice President, Ellett &
Short, Inc.)

Cassidy, James A.
(Chairman of the Board,
James A. Cassidy Co. Inc.)

Caulfield, Dr. Philip A.
(Physician-Surgeon)

Christie, John M.
(Senior Vice President,
Riggs National Bank)

Clarke, Hon. Edward J.
(Minority Whip, House of
Delegates, Md.)

Collins, Dr. William J.
(Physician)

Connolly, Paul R.
(Attorney-at-Law)

Corcoran, Hon. Howard F.
(Judge, U.S. District Court,
District of Columbia)

Corcoran, Thomas G.
(Attorney-at-Law)

Coughlin, Paul H.
(President, Overseas
Service Corp.)

Crowley, Louis P.
(Vice president, Walker &
Dunlop, Inc.)

Cullen, John B.
(Attorney-at-Law)

Curran, Hon. Edward M.
(Chief Judge, U.S. District
Court, District of Columbia)

Curran, Edward M., Jr.
(Chesapeake & Potomac
Telephone Co.,
Hyattsville, Md.)

Davis, F. Elwood
(Attorney-at-Law)

Dempsey, William J.
(Attorney-at-Law)

Donahue, John F.
Vice President, Hohenstein
Bros. & Donahue, Inc.)

Donovan, Dr. Leo I.
(Physician)

Doulens, Roger B.
(Asst. Vice President,
Pan American World
Airways)

Downey, Fred M.
(Executive Vice President,
Peoples Drug Stores, Inc.)

Dunn, R. Roy
(Chairman of the Board,
Potomac Electric Power Co.)

Ferguson, Francis J.
(Attorney-at-Law)

Fitzgerald, Dr. James Edward
(Physician)

Flanagan, Francis D.
(Asst. Vice President,
W. R. Grace & Co.)

Fleming, Robert W.
(Executive Vice President
& Secretary,
Folger, Nolan, Fleming & Co.)

Foley, Hon. Edward H.
(Attorney-at-Law)

Folliard, Edward T.
(Retired Newspaperman)

Furey, E. William
(Attorney-at-Law)

Gallagher, Dr. John P.
(Neuro-Surgeon)

Garrity, Raymond F.
(Attorney-at-Law)

Gerrity, Harry J.
(Attorney-at-Law)

Gibbs, Frederick R.
(Attorney-at-Law)

Glenn, Rev. Dr. C. Leslie,
S.T.D.
(Canon, Washington
National Cathedral)

Hickey, Edward J., Jr.
(Attorney-at-Law)

Jackson, Hon. Joseph R.
(Retired Judge—U.S. District
Court)

Johnston, Hon. Felton M.
(Retired Former Secretary
of the U.S. Senate)

Jones, Hon. William B.
(Judge, U.S. District Court,
District of Columbia)

Kacy, Howard W.
(Chairman of the Board,
Acacia Mutual Life
Insurance Co.)

Kane, Al. Philip
(Attorney-at-Law)

Kane, Francis J.
(President, Kane Transfer
Company)

Kane, Harry J., Jr.
(President, The Columbia
Real Estate Title
Insurance Co.)

Kane, Matthew A.
(Attorney-at-Law)

Keane, Thomas T.
(Vice President, Washington
Beef Company, Inc.)

Kennedy, Dr. Joseph W.
(Physician)

Kennedy, Dr. Michael
(Physician)

Kenney, Hon. W. John
(Attorney-at-Law)

Keogh, Michael F.
(Attorney-at-Law)

Kreglow, Dr. Alan Frank
(Physician)

McArdle, Paul F.
(Attorney-at-Law)

McCabe, Edward A.
(Attorney-at-Law)

McDermott, Edward A.
(Attorney-at-Law)

McGarraghy, Alfred A.
(Operator, The Shrine
Cafeteria, National Shrine of
the Immaculate Conception)

McGarraghy, Hon. Joseph C.
(Judge, U.S. District Court,
District of Columbia)

McGuire, Hon. Matthew F.
(Judge, U.S. District Court,
District of Columbia)

McGuirk, Dr. James J.
(Physician)

McHugh, Hon. Simon F., Jr.
(Member, Subversive
Activities Control Board)

McInerney, Martin
(Real Estate Broker)

McInerney, Maurice F.
(Real Estate Broker)

McLaughlin, Hon. Charles F.
(Judge, U.S. District Court,
District of Columbia)

McLeod, William N., Jr.
(Public Relations)

McManus, William J.
(Retired)

McNamara, Dr. C. Edwin
(Physician)

McNamara, Martin J.
(Special Counsel to the Vice
President of the United
States)

Mack, Corneal J.
(Vice President &
Managing Director
The Mayflower Hotel)

Mahar, Richard A.
(Attorney-at-Law)

Maher, Daniel B.
(Attorney-at-Law)

Martens, Harry Jr.
(Chairman of the Board,
L. P. Steuart Organizations)

Meehan, Robert M.
(Seafood Broker)

Millwater, Dr. Charles A.
(Physician)

Murphy, H. Gabriel
(President, H. Gabriel
Murphy & Company)

Murray, Dr. Francis M.
(Dental Surgeon)

Murray, Joseph L. B.
(Insurance Broker & Agent)

Nealon, Dr. Stephen W., Jr.
(Physician)

O'Brien, Dan J.
(Adm. Assistant to
Senator Hickenlooper)

O'Connor, George H.
(Public Relations)

O'Connor, William J.
(President, Southern
Wholesalers, Inc.)

O'Donoghue, Daniel W.
(Attorney-at-Law)

O'Donoghue, Martin F.
(Attorney-at-Law)

Quinn, Arthur L.
(Attorney-at-Law)

Quinn, Arthur Lee
(Attorney-at-Law)

Quinn, Hon. Thomas Dewey
(Associate Judge, District of
Columbia Court of Appeals)

Quinn, Thomas D., Jr.
(Attorney-at-Law)

Reilly, James F.
(Attorney-at-Law)

Reilly, James Francis
(Attorney-at-Law)

Reilly, Martin L.
(President, Marty Reilly
Company)

Riley, Joseph H.
(Senior Vice President,
National Savings & Trust Co.)

Rowe, James H., Jr.
(Attorney-at-Law)

Sanderson, Dr. Fred R.
(Physician)

Saul, B. Francis II
(Senior Vice President,
B. F. Saul & Company)

Scalley, Hon. Thomas C.
(Judge, D. C. Court of
General Sessions)

Shannon, William E.
(Chairman of the Board,
Shannon & Luchs Company)

Shea, John E.
(Attorney-at-Law)

Smith, Hon. John Lewis, Jr.
(Judge, U.S. District Court,
District of Columbia)

Steele, Charles J.
(Attorney-at-Law)

Stohlman, Frederick
(Attorney-at-Law)

Sullivan, Hon. John L.
(Attorney-at-Law)

Tamm, Hon. Edward A.
  (Judge, U.S. Court of
  Appeals, D. C. Circuit)

Thom, Corcoran, Jr.
  (Senior Vice President,
  Riggs National Bank)

Tumulty, Joseph P., Jr.
  (Attorney-at-Law)

Vinson, Hon. Fred M., Jr.
  (Assistant United States
  Attorney General)

Walsh, Dr. Bernard J.
  (Physician)

Walsh, Richard T.
  (President, Federated
  Insurance Agencies, Inc.)

Walsh, Thomas M.
  (President, Thomas D.
  Walsh, Inc.)

Woll, J. Albert
  (General Counsel AFL-CIO)

HONORARY MEMBERS

Hon. William J. Brennan, Jr.
Hon. Dwight D. Eisenhower
Hon. William P. Fay
Mr. Bernard T. Fitzgerald
Hon. George A. Garrett
Rev. Gilbert V. Hartke, O.P.
Hon. John J. Hearne
Hon. Lyndon B. Johnson
Hon. Sean Nunan
Patrick Cardinal O'Boyle
Hon. Harry S. Truman
Hon. J. Russell Young
Hon. Earl Warren

NON-RESIDENT MEMBERS

H. Loy Anderson
William F. Cruise
Thomas J. Mangan
Rt. Rev. Msgr. Joseph McShea
L. Gardner Moore
Edgar L. Morris
Martin J. O'Connell
Thomas E. Stephens
George M. Quirk

ASSOCIATE MEMBERS

Dr. Robert Howe Harmon
Sampson P. Holland
William D. Jones
Arthur W. McCoy
Raymond M. McGuire
Walter F. McArdle
William D. McIntyre
Frank J. Martell
James A. Mulroe
Robert C. Nicholson
Leo Patrick Payton
J. Benton Webb
Thomas V. Whelan

NECROLOGY

Atkinson, Rev. Dr. George W.
Beavers, Thomas N.
Bell, Charles J.
Bell, John G.
Biggs, Dr. J. Rozier
Bland, Hon. Oscar E.
Boland, Thornton
Bowie, John F. M.
Brahany, Hon. Thomas W.
Browning, William L.
Burkinshaw, Neil
Cahill, Dr. James A.
Cahill, Robert F.
Callahan, Daniel J.
Cantwell, Thomas A.
Cavanaugh, Rev. Francis X.
Claggett, William H.
Clark, Charles Patrick
Colliflower, James E.
Cooke, Levi
Cotter, Joseph J.
Cromelin, Paul R.
Crosson, Dr. Henry J.
Crowley, John T.
Crowley, Thomas R.
Cummings, Andrew J.
Darr, Charles W.
Delacy, Hon. William
Dunigan, David J.
Dunn, J. S.
East, Fred
Euwer, Walter Courtney
Fleming, Robert V.
Foote, Dr. John
Furey, William E.
Gaffney, Dr. Leo B.
Gibbs, M. G.
Goldsborough, Hon. T. Alan
Greaney, John F.
Groom, Thomas J.
Guider, John W.
Guilday, Rev. Dr. Peter
Haley, Andrew G.
Handy, Levin P.
Harlow, Leo P.
Healey, Rev. Dr. Patrick J.
Hogan, Frank J.
Horne, Matthew
Horning, Joseph F.
Johansen, Edward H.
Kennedy, Hon. William P.
Leahy, William E.
Lenihan, Hon. James J.
Lennox, Dr. P. I.
Locraft, Thomas H.
Long, Maurice G.
Lowe, Dr. Thomas
McAtee, Camden R.

McCann, George E.
McCann, Robert C.
McCormick, Michael G.
McGovern, James P.
McGuire, Chester J.
McHugh, Simon F.
McInerney, John J.
McInerney, Dr. Michael J.
McLaughlin, Rev. Dr. Peter J.
McMahon, Hon. Brian
McNally, William J.
McNamara, Most Rev. John M.
McNamara, Martin J.
McQuade, Edward J.
Monaghan, Joseph C.
Montgomery, Robert B.
Montgomery, William
Moran, Charles P. L.
Morris, Edgar
Mullen, Arthur F.
Murphy, Fred A.
Murray, Dr. Joseph L. B.
Noonan, John J.
Norris, Dr. L. B.
Norton, Robert
O'Brien, Col. Arthur
O'Connor, George H.
O'Connor, William E.
O'Donnell, Dr. William F.
O'Dwyer, Rev. Dr. David F.
O'Hara, Frank
Payne, Lewis A.
Quinn, Henry I.
Reilly, Hugh
Reilly, Hugh, Jr.
Reilly, John A.
Ryan, Most Rev. James Hugh
Saul, John
Shahan, Rt. Rev. Thomas J.
Shea, Dennis C.
Shea, George F.
Shea, James McD.
Sherley, Hon. Swagar
Slattery, Thomas F.
Somerville, Harry P.
Stanley, Hon. A. O.
Stanton, Dr. William J.
Steuart, L. P.
Sullivan, James A.
Sullivan, Jos. D.
Thom, Corcoran
Toland, Edmund M.
Tumulty, Hon. Joseph P.
Vandoren, Lucien J.
Vinson, Hon. Fred M.
Walsh, Edward J.
Walsh, John
Weller, Francis R.

OFFICERS OF THE SOCIETY

April 25, 1928

President—Colonel Arthur O'Brien

First Vice President—Herbert T. Shannon

Second Vice President—William E. Leahy

Treasurer—Daniel J. O'Brien

Secretary—Milton E. Ailes, Jr.

Historian—

1929

Colonel Arthur O'Brien
Herbert T. Shannon
William E. Leahy
Daniel J. O'Brien
Milton E. Ailes, Jr.

1929-1930

Colonel Arthur O'Brien
Dr. Charles E. O'Connor
William C. Sullivan
Daniel J. O'Brien
Martin J. McNamara
William P. Kennedy

1930-1931

Colonel Arthur O'Brien
Joseph P. Tumulty
William C. Sullivan
Daniel J. O'Brien
Martin J. McNamara
William P. Kennedy

1931-1932

Colonel Arthur O'Brien
Joseph P. Tumulty
William C. Sullivan
Daniel J. O'Brien
Martin J. McNamara
William P. Kennedy

1932-1933

Colonel Arthur O'Brien
William C. Sullivan
George H. O'Connor
Daniel J. O'Brien
Martin J. McNamara
William P. Kennedy

1933-1934

Colonel Arthur O'Brien
William C. Sullivan
George H. O'Connor
Daniel J. O'Brien
Martin J. McNamara
William P. Kennedy

1934-1935

Colonel Arthur O'Brien
William C. Sullivan
George H. O'Connor
Daniel J. O'Brien
Martin J. McNamara
William P. Kennedy

1935-1936

Colonel Arthur O'Brien
George H. O'Connor
William Montgomery
Thomas R. Crowley
Martin J. McNamara
William P. Kennedy

1936-1937

Colonel Arthur O'Brien
George H. O'Connor
William Montgomery
Thomas R. Crowley
William P. Kennedy
Martin J. McNamara

1937-1938

Daniel J. Callahan
George H. O'Connor
John W. Guider
Thomas R. Crowley
Martin J. McNamara
William P. Kennedy

1938-1939

George H. O'Connor
Dr. H. J. Crosson
Malcolm G. Gibbs
Michael F. Calnan
Martin J. McNamara
William P. Kennedy

1939-1940

Dr. H. J. Crosson
Malcolm G. Gibbs
John Saul
Michael F. Calnan
Martin J. McNamara
William P. Kennedy

1940-1941

Malcolm G. Gibbs
John Saul
Thomas W. Brahany
Michael F. Calnan
Martin J. McNamara
William P. Kennedy

1941-1942

John Saul
Thomas W. Brahany
Dr. Edward Larkin
Michael F. Calnan
Martin J. McNamara
William P. Kennedy

1942-1943

Thomas W. Brahany
Dr. Edward Larkin
William Montgomery
Martin J. McNamara
Michael F. Calnan
William P. Kennedy

1943-1944

Dr. Edward Larkin
William Montgomery
James E. Colliflower
Michael F. Calnan
Martin J. McNamara
William P. Kennedy

1944-1945

William Montgomery
James E. Colliflower
William E. Leahy
Michael F. Calnan
Martin J. McNamara
William P. Kennedy

1945-1946

James E. Colliflower
William E. Leahy
John G. Bell
Michael F. Calnan
Martin J. McNamara
William P. Kennedy

1946-1947

William E. Leahy
John G. Bell
Dr. Fred Sanderson
Daniel J. Callahan, Jr.
Martin J. McNamara
William P. Kennedy

1947-1948

John G. Bell
Dr. Fred Sanderson
John A. Reilly
Daniel J. Callahan, Jr.
Simon F. McHugh
William P. Kennedy

1948-1949

Dr. Fred R. Sanderson
John A. Reilly
Edgar Morris
Daniel J. Callahan, Jr.
Simon F. McHugh
William P. Kennedy

1949-1950

John A. Reilly
Edgar Morris
Francis J. Kane
Daniel J. Callahan, Jr.
Simon F. McHugh
William P. Kennedy

1950-1951

Edgar Morris
Francis J. Kane
Dr. Philip A. Caulfield
Daniel J. Callahan, Jr.
Simon F. McHugh
William P. Kennedy

1951-1952

Francis J. Kane
Dr. Philip A. Caulfield
Howard W. Kacy
Daniel J. Callahan, Jr.
Simon F. McHugh
William P. Kennedy

1952-1953

Dr. Philip A. Caulfield
Howard W. Kacy
Corneal J. Mack
Daniel J. Callahan, Jr.
Simon F. McHugh
William P. Kennedy

1953-1954

Howard W. Kacy
Corneal J. Mack
Joseph P. Tumulty, Jr.
Daniel J. Callahan, Jr.
Simon F. McHugh
William P. Kennedy

1954-1955

Corneal J. Mack
Joseph P. Tumulty, Jr.
L. P. Steuart
Daniel J. Callahan, Jr.
Simon F. McHugh
Edward T. Folliard

1955-1956

Joseph P. Tumulty, Jr.
L. P. Steuart
James A. Cassidy
Daniel J. Callahan, Jr.
Simon F. McHugh
Edward T. Folliard

1956-1957

L. P. Steuart
James A. Cassidy
James Francis Reilly
Daniel J. Callahan, Jr.
Simon F. McHugh
Edward T. Folliard

1957-1958

James A. Cassidy
James Francis Reilly
Robert V. Fleming
Daniel J. Callahan, Jr.
Simon F. McHugh
Edward T. Folliard

1958-1959	1959-1960
James Francis Reilly	Robert V. Fleming
Robert V. Fleming	John J. Carmody
John J. Carmody	Raymond F. Garrity
Daniel J. Callahan, Jr.	Daniel J. Callahan, Jr.
Simon F .McHugh	Simon F. McHugh
Edward T. Folliard	Edward T. Folliard

1960-1961	1961-1962
John J. Carmody	Raymond F. Garrity
Raymond F. Garrity	George B. Burrus
George B. Burrus	Daniel J. Callahan, Jr.
Daniel J. Callahan, Jr.	John B. Cullen
Simon F. McHugh	Simon F. McHugh
Edward T. Folliard	Edward T. Folliard

1962-1963	1963-1964
George B. Burrus	Daniel J. Callahan, Jr.
Daniel J. Callahan, Jr.	Hon. Edward M. Curran
Hon. Edward M. Curran	Rev. C. Leslie Glenn, S.T.D.
John B. Cullen	John B. Cullen
Simon F. McHugh	Simon F. McHugh
Edward T. Folliard	Edward T. Folliard

1964-1965	1965-1966
Hon. Edward M. Curran	Rev. C. Leslie Glenn, S.T.D.
Rev. C. Leslie Glenn, S.T.D.	Hon. Edward A. Tamm
Hon. Edward A. Tamm	Arthur L. Quinn
Gerald K. Cassidy	Gerald K. Cassidy
John B. Cullen	John B. Cullen
Edward T. Folliard	Edward T. Folliard

1966-1967	1967-1968
Arthur L. Quinn	Hon. William B. Jones
Hon. William B. Jones	Robert W. Fleming
William J. McManus	Hon. John L. Sullivan
Gerald K. Cassidy	Gerald K. Cassidy
John B. Cullen	John B. Cullen
Edward T. Folliard	Edward T. Folliard

THE HAIL OF THE FRIENDLY SONS

Come, raise the brimming cup on high
Across the festive board,
And pledge the ancient troth once more
And quaff the fabled gourd!
A hail to God and Country—
To all that's good and true—
A hail to all that we hold dear,
A hail to me and you!
A hail to freemen everywhere
For nothing else remains
And Irish hearts in outrage, pulse,
When Freedom lies in chains!
And now a hail to Patrick
While the stirrup cup still runs—
And a rousing, great "God Bless You!"
From the hearts of his Friendly Sons.

MATTHEW F. MCGUIRE

THE PAST IS PROLOGUE

In the spring of 1968, the Society embarked on its Forty-First year with the election of Robert W. (Bus) Fleming as President. He thus follows in the footsteps of his father, Robert V. Fleming, long Washington's most famous banker, who served as the Society's president in 1960. May the past 40 years foretell of greater things for our Society, our City, and our Country in the next Forty.

www.ingramcontent.com/pod-product-compliance
Lightning Source LLC
Chambersburg PA
CBHW031617040426
42452CB00006B/567